THIS BOOK IS FOR

··

BORN

··

LOTS OF LOVE
FORVER & ALWAYS

··

On the day you were born

Date: Weight:

Day of the week: Length:

Time of birth: Eyes:

Place of birth: Hair:

The person who delivered you:

The first people you met:

You were very close to being called   or

Other runner up names:

The weather was:

The biggest headline in the news was:

The number one song was:

My favorite song at the moment (& the song you probably heard
most in my tummy:

My first impressions of you & how I felt Immediately after your
birth:

The story of bringing you home from the hospital that day:

Here are a few things you should know about your family:

All the things I hope for your future:

The world I want to give you:

Newborn baby memories

Newborn baby memories

Happy Birthday

1

To my dearest

What we did to celebrate your birthday:

This last year has been:

Some of my fondest memories:

The trips/vacations we took were:

This year you learnt how to:

Things you loved this year:

Things you didn't like as much:

Milestones:

Changes that have happened over the past year:

Things I have learnt about myself this year:

The best advise I can give you at this point in time:

♪ This years most played songs ♫

Mine

☆
☆
☆
☆

Yours

☆
☆
☆
☆

My wishes and hopes for the next year:

Memories

Happy Birthday

2

To my dearest

What we did to celebrate your birthday:

This last year has been:

Some of my fondest memories:

The trips/vacations we took were:

This year you learnt how to:

Things you loved this year:

Things you didn't like as much:

Milestones:

Changes that have happened over the past year:

Things I have learnt about myself this year:

The best advise I can give you at this point in time:

This years most played songs

Mine | Yours
☆ | ☆
☆ | ☆
☆ | ☆
☆ | ☆

My wishes and hopes for the next year:

Memories

Happy Birthday

3

To my dearest

What we did to celebrate your birthday:

This last year has been:

Some of my fondest memories:

The trips/vacations we took were:

This year you learnt how to:

Things you loved this year:

Things you didn't like as much:

Milestones:

Changes that have happened over the past year:

Things I have learnt about myself this year:

The best advise I can give you at this point in time:

𝄞 This years most played songs ♫

Mine	Yours
☆	☆
☆	☆
☆	☆
☆	☆

My wishes and hopes for the next year:

Memories

Happy Birthday

4

To my dearest

What we did to celebrate your birthday:

This last year has been:

Some of my fondest memories:

The trips/vacations we took were:

This year you learnt how to:

Things you loved this year:

Things you didn't like as much:

Milestones:

Changes that have happened over the past year:

Things I have learnt about myself this year:

The best advise I can give you at this point in time:

𝄞 This years most played songs ♫

Mine   Yours
☆   ☆

☆   ☆

☆   ☆

☆   ☆

My wishes and hopes for the next year:

Memories

Happy Birthday

5

To my dearest

What we did to celebrate your birthday:

This last year has been:

Some of my fondest memories:

The trips/vacations we took were:

This year you learnt how to:

Things you loved this year:

Things you didn't like as much:

Milestones:

Changes that have happened over the past year:

Things I have learnt about myself this year:

The best advise I can give you at this point in time:

𝄞 *This years most played songs* ♫

Mine	Yours
☆	☆
☆	☆
☆	☆
☆	☆

My wishes and hopes for the next year:

Memories

Happy Birthday

To my dearest

What we did to celebrate your birthday:

This last year has been:

Some of my fondest memories:

The trips/vacations we took were:

This year you learnt how to:

Things you loved this year:

Things you didn't like as much:

Milestones:

Changes that have happened over the past year:

Things I have learnt about myself this year:

The best advise I can give you at this point in time:

𝄞 *This years most played songs* ♫

Mine   Yours
☆   ☆

☆   ☆

☆   ☆

☆   ☆

My wishes and hopes for the next year:

Memories

Happy Birthday

7

To my dearest

What we did to celebrate your birthday:

This last year has been:

Some of my fondest memories:

The trips/vacations we took were:

This year you learnt how to:

Things you loved this year:

Things you didn't like as much:

Milestones:

Changes that have happened over the past year:

Things I have learnt about myself this year:

The best advise I can give you at this point in time:

♪ This years most played songs ♫

Mine   Yours
☆   ☆

☆   ☆

☆   ☆

☆   ☆

My wishes and hopes for the next year:

Memories

Happy Birthday

8

To my dearest

What we did to celebrate your birthday:

This last year has been:

Some of my fondest memories:

The trips/vacations we took were:

This year you learnt how to:

Things you loved this year:

Things you didn't like as much:

Milestones:

Changes that have happened over the past year:

Things I have learnt about myself this year:

The best advise I can give you at this point in time:

♪ This years most played songs ♫

Mine	Yours
☆	☆
☆	☆
☆	☆
☆	☆

My wishes and hopes for the next year:

Memories

Happy Birthday

9

To my dearest

What we did to celebrate your birthday:

This last year has been:

Some of my fondest memories:

The trips/vacations we took were:

This year you learnt how to:

Things you loved this year:

Things you didn't like as much:

Milestones:

Changes that have happened over the past year:

Things I have learnt about myself this year:

The best advise I can give you at this point in time:

♪ This years most played songs ♫

Mine	Yours
☆	☆
☆	☆
☆	☆
☆	☆

My wishes and hopes for the next year:

Memories

Happy Birthday

10

To my dearest

What we did to celebrate your birthday:

This last year has been:

Some of my fondest memories:

The trips/vacations we took were:

This year you learnt how to:

Things you loved this year:

Things you didn't like as much:

Milestones:

Changes that have happened over the past year:

Things I have learnt about myself this year:

The best advise I can give you at this point in time:

𝄞 *This years most played songs* ♫

Mine

☆

☆

☆

☆

Yours

☆

☆

☆

☆

My wishes and hopes for the next year:

Memories

Happy Birthday

11

To my dearest

What we did to celebrate your birthday:

This last year has been:

Some of my fondest memories:

The trips/vacations we took were:

This year you learnt how to:

Things you loved this year:

Things you didn't like as much:

Milestones:

Changes that have happened over the past year:

Things I have learnt about myself this year:

The best advise I can give you at this point in time:

This years most played songs

Mine   Yours

☆   ☆

☆   ☆

☆   ☆

☆   ☆

My wishes and hopes for the next year:

Memories

Happy Birthday

12

To my dearest

What we did to celebrate your birthday:

This last year has been:

Some of my fondest memories:

The trips/vacations we took were:

This year you learnt how to:

Things you loved this year:

Things you didn't like as much:

Milestones:

Changes that have happened over the past year:

Things I have learnt about myself this year:

The best advise I can give you at this point in time:

𝄞 *This years most played songs* ♫

Mine

☆

☆

☆

☆

Yours

☆

☆

☆

☆

My wishes and hopes for the next year:

Memories

Happy Birthday

13

To my dearest

What we did to celebrate your birthday:

This last year has been:

Some of my fondest memories:

The trips/vacations we took were:

This year you learnt how to:

Things you loved this year:

Things you didn't like as much:

Milestones:

Changes that have happened over the past year:

Things I have learnt about myself this year:

The best advise I can give you at this point in time:

This years most played songs ♫

Mine	Yours
☆	☆
☆	☆
☆	☆
☆	☆

My wishes and hopes for the next year:

Memories

Happy Birthday

14

To my dearest

What we did to celebrate your birthday:

This last year has been:

Some of my fondest memories:

The trips/vacations we took were:

This year you learnt how to:

Things you loved this year:

Things you didn't like as much:

Milestones:

Changes that have happened over the past year:

Things I have learnt about myself this year:

The best advise I can give you at this point in time:

This years most played songs ♫

Mine   Yours
☆   ☆
☆   ☆
☆   ☆
☆   ☆

My wishes and hopes for the next year:

Memories

Happy Birthday

15

To my dearest

What we did to celebrate your birthday:

This last year has been:

Some of my fondest memories:

The trips/vacations we took were:

This year you learnt how to:

Things you loved this year:

Things you didn't like as much:

Milestones:

Changes that have happened over the past year:

Things I have learnt about myself this year:

The best advise I can give you at this point in time:

♪ *This years most played songs* ♫

Mine   Yours
☆   ☆
☆   ☆
☆   ☆
☆   ☆

My wishes and hopes for the next year:

Memories

Happy Birthday

16

To my dearest

What we did to celebrate your birthday:

This last year has been:

Some of my fondest memories:

The trips/vacations we took were:

This year you learnt how to:

Things you loved this year:

Things you didn't like as much:

Milestones:

Changes that have happened over the past year:

Things I have learnt about myself this year:

The best advise I can give you at this point in time:

𝄞 *This years most played songs* ♫

Mine | Yours
☆ | ☆
☆ | ☆
☆ | ☆
☆ | ☆

My wishes and hopes for the next year:

Memories

Happy Birthday 17

To my dearest

What we did to celebrate your birthday:

This last year has been:

Some of my fondest memories:

The trips/vacations we took were:

This year you learnt how to:

Things you loved this year:

Things you didn't like as much:

Milestones:

Changes that have happened over the past year:

Things I have learnt about myself this year:

The best advise I can give you at this point in time:

♪ This years most played songs ♫

Mine

☆

☆

☆

☆

Yours

☆

☆

☆

☆

My wishes and hopes for the next year:

Memories

Happy Birthday

18

To my dearest

What we did to celebrate your birthday:

This last year has been:

Some of my fondest memories:

The trips/vacations we took were:

This year you learnt how to:

Things you loved this year:

Things you didn't like as much:

Milestones:

Changes that have happened over the past year:

Things I have learnt about myself this year:

The best advise I can give you at this point in time:

𝄞 This years most played songs ♫

Mine	Yours
☆	☆
☆	☆
☆	☆
☆	☆

My wishes and hopes for you:

Now that you are an adult (Kind of)

Be prepared to:

Always keep:

Focus on:

Never:

Always remember:

Be Open to:

Surround yourself with:

I wish you:

One last thing:

Memories

Memories

Memories

Made in United States
Orlando, FL
05 October 2022

23025603R00067